This September 1950 wedding portrait was taken at the reception given by the bride's parents, Mr. and Mrs. Andrew J. Dancy, at their home on Edith Street. The newlyweds, Charles and Anita Wallace, are seated in front of the fireplace on the left. The bridge's sister, Frances Dancy (far left), served as the maid-of-honor. The groom graduated from Howard University Medical School and was a member of the Kappa Alpha Psi fraternity. Anita, a member of the Alpha Kapa Alpha sorority, also graduated from Howard University. (Mississippi Valley Collection.)

ON THE COVER: The Hooks brothers successfully operated one of the leading photography studios in Memphis during much of the 20th century. They chronicled the Memphis black community from 1907 until the 1970s, documenting businesses, church groups, street scenes, homes, schools, weddings, portraits, entertainers, and more. The entire view of this 1950s wedding portrait is shown above. (Mississippi Valley Collection.)

IMAGES
of America

AFRICAN AMERICANS
IN MEMPHIS

Earnestine Lovelle Jenkins

ARCADIA
PUBLISHING

Published by Arcadia Publishing
Charleston, South Carolina

Library of Congress Control Number: 2008942948

For all general information contact Arcadia Publishing at:
Telephone 843-853-2070
Fax 843-853-0044
E-mail sales@arcadiapublishing.com
For customer service and orders:
Toll-Free 1-888-313-2665

Visit us on the Internet at www.arcadiapublishing.com

To my mother, Lovelle Fouse Jenkins (1923–2007),
whose love and knowledge of Memphis and its people, her family,
friends, and professional colleagues continues to inspire.

CONTENTS

ACKNOWLEDGMENTS

I would like to thank a number of individuals and institutions that supported this project. While archive collections are noted in the credit lines, I owe a special thanks to Ed Frank and the library staff in the Special Collection at the University of Memphis Ned McWherter Library; Margaret McNutt at the Pink Palace Museum; and the librarians who were so patient with my repeated requests to research photographs in the Memphis Room at the Benjamin Hooks Library. I also owe a special thanks to Dr. Benjamin Hooks, who granted permission to use the Hooks Brothers photographs, as the Hooks family retains copyrights to this material. I also thank Diane Wright and Wilford Glenn for access to their private collections. In addition, thanks to Richard Lou and Jason Miller of the Department of Art at the University of Memphis for their support of the 2008 art exhibit Early African American Photographers in Memphis.

INTRODUCTION

During the Civil War, escaped slaves fled rural plantations, seeking refuge in Memphis. By the war's end, 17,000 blacks had settled in the city, numbers too significant for whites to ignore. Violence erupted in the race riot of 1866. White mobs went on a three-day rampage, killing 46 blacks, raping black women, and burning churches, homes, and schools.

It was not enough to drive the newly freed away. The emancipated continued to set down roots in Memphis, creating the communities that sustained them after slavery. They founded neighborhoods and proceeded to build homes, churches, schools, and cemeteries in which to bury their dead with respect. Benevolent societies were organized to care for the elderly and orphans, while hospitals were constructed to provide health care. Black newspapers and journalists reported and discussed information important to the fledgling communities.

A class of professionals was drawn to the largest urban center in the Mid-South, providing services to Memphis's growing black population as lawyers, doctors, pharmacists, teachers and principals, trained musicians, and educated clergy. Most migrant men found work as laborers, while women found jobs as domestic workers. Some were able to move up economically by establishing barbershops and hair salons, working as tailors or seamstresses, operating a saloon, grocery store, or boardinghouse, and buying real estate.

Black Memphians struggled to procure their civil rights. In 1892, the lynching of three black businessmen drove Ida B. Wells to publicly condemn this type of domestic terrorism. She never returned to Memphis after her life was threatened, and many others followed suit. The violence of the post-Reconstruction South caused another black female leader in Memphis, Julia Britton Hooks, to write an influential essay entitled "The Duty of the Hour," published in the 1895 *Afro-American Encyclopedia*. Julia Hooks used the example of Memphis to urge African Americans to stand fast in the face of racial violence.

By the end of the 19th century, African Americans had won hard-fought victories and achievements for their race. Memphis was home to a new, urban, 20th-century community. Much of this early vibrant African American culture was centered on Beale Street, the epicenter of black political, social, religious, and economic life. Up until the late 1940s, Beale Street thrived with its churches, banks, barbershops, and doctor's offices; clothing stores, theaters, restaurants, saloons, and drugstores; as well as gambling dens, juke joints, fraternal clubs, and entertainment agencies. Robert R. Church, W. C. Handy, and George W. Lee were the proclaimed leaders of Beale, but it was equally the prized possession of its sporting men, showgirls, cooks and maids, street corner preachers, gamblers, voodoo practitioners, and roustabouts. Most of the early black businesses in Memphis first opened in the Beale Street area, such as Solvent Bank and Trust Company in 1906, Hooks Brothers Photographers in 1907, and Emma Wilburn Funeral Home in 1914. Through it all, African American life and culture was anchored by Beale Street Baptist Church. The "Mother Church" still overlooks the famous street from her twin towers and stained-glass windows at 169 Beale Street.

The 1940s and 1950s brought changes that prepared the way for the civil rights movement. African Americans in Memphis participated in World War II and the Korean War, and benefitted from

their service to the country. While they lived in one of the most segregated cities in the United States, black men and women challenged racial, class, and gender inequalities. They protested police brutality and job discrimination, and began to campaign for political office.

While African Americans in Memphis may have been physically locked in, so to speak, segregation failed to reign in black culture. Black cultural development in Memphis reflected the black struggle. The phenomenon of WDIA radio, rhythm and blues music, the literary and visual arts, gospel, schools, neighborhoods, clubs, and everyday lifestyle in general were all influenced by an increasing political consciousness. This book is a visual history, a look at how African Americans in Memphis lived through emancipation, segregation, and the onset of the civil rights movement.

One

MEMPHIS PIONEERS
SLAVES, FREE PEOPLE, AND MIGRANTS

During the early 1800s, Memphis developed into an important destination for black and white migrants. The city's growth as the political and economic hub of the upper Mississippi Valley was tied to cotton, slavery, and transportation. By the mid-19th century, Memphis was the largest inland slave-trading center in the South. Black labor was critical to the success of Memphis as a trading center. There were about 3,338 slaves in the city by 1860 and 198 freed blacks. The bulk of the slave population in West Tennessee worked in the rural counties surrounding Memphis. The urban slave population in the city worked as laborers, draymen, mechanics, craftsmen, domestic servants, cooks, and washerwomen. (Memphis Room.)

The Civil War was the catalyst that dramatically changed the demographics of the Memphis population. Escaped slaves fled rural plantations, seeking refuge in Memphis. By the war's end, 17,000 blacks had settled in the city. Many of the new migrants settled in the downtown area around Linden, Beale, Turley, Causey, and St. Martin Streets. Some whites referred to this new community as the "Negro Quarters." Here were located all the elements of community building, including hotels, groceries, churches, and schools alongside poor, overcrowded, and unsanitary living conditions. Blacks were often at odds with the Irish immigrant population living in the same neighborhoods in similar conditions. With the addition of African American soldiers serving with the 3rd U.S. Colored Heavy Artillery, the mix was ripe for explosion. Violence erupted in the race riot of 1866. (Private collection.)

The story of Lucy Jane Wright and her family illustrates the multiethnic history of Indian, black, and white relations in early-19th-century Memphis. The Wright family is one of the earliest documented families of color with roots in Memphis, arriving before the Civil War. Lucy Jane Wright's mother, Ann, was Afro-Indian. The family remained in Memphis after the forced exodus of Native Americans from the Mid-South, known as the Trail of Tears, in 1837. Chickasaw and Choctaw from the area marched with many other Native Americans along Adams Street to the docks, where they got on boats taking them to reservations in Oklahoma and other points west. Ann, described as Benjamin Wright's Afro-Indian housekeeper, was one of the few free or enslaved women in Memphis living in common-law relations with white men. Intolerant of interracial relationships, the city passed an ordinance prohibiting white men from keeping "colored" wives in 1837. However, Ann had already borne Wright twin daughters named Eliza Frances (left) and Lucy Jane Wright (right) in 1835. (Mississippi Valley Collection.)

Benjamin Wright was from a Quaker family in Philadelphia. He owned a plantation and general store near Memphis. The family lived in a two-story home on Front Street, a site later occupied by the Shelby County jail. Before his death, Benjamin took Ann and his daughters to Cairo, Illinois, to establish their freedom, after which the family returned to Memphis. (Mississippi Valley Collection.)

Lucy Jane Wright (1835–1906) became a pioneer businesswoman. She supported her family by managing rental properties and working as a skilled seamstress. Her diversity of friends included prosperous Chinese merchant Joe Pang and his wife, and Jacob Goldsmith of the department store family. Memphians gathered in her parlor for political discussions. When Frederick Douglass visited Memphis, he was a guest in Wright's home on Hernando and Beale Streets. (Mississippi Valley Collection.)

Col. James Coleman was the father of Lucy Jane Wright's three children, Anna, Benjamin, and James. He lived in Memphis for several years and managed the telegraph office, where the famous inventor Thomas Edison briefly worked. Edison's letter is in response to an inquiry from Anna Wright. (Mississippi Valley Collection.)

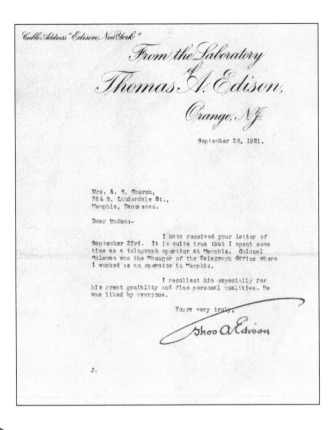

From the Laboratory of Thomas A. Edison, Orange, N.J.

September 28, 1921.

Mrs. A. S. Church,
784 S. Lauderdale St.,
Memphis, Tennessee.

Dear Madam:-

      I have received your letter of September 23rd. It is quite true that I spent some time as a telegraph operator at Memphis. Colonel Coleman was the Manager of the Telegraph Office where I worked as an operator in Memphis.

      I recollect him especially for his great geniality and fine personal qualities. He was liked by everyone.

Yours very truly,

Thos A Edison

Anna Wright Church (1856–1928) became an accomplished musician and respected city school principal. Lucy Jane Wright enrolled Anna in Lemoyne Normal Institute. In 1876, she was one of the two members of the school's first graduating class. Wright also hired German professors to instruct Anna in piano lessons. She attended Antioch College in Yellow Springs, Ohio, and after returning to Memphis, she taught school, then became principal of Auction Street School. Anna married the wealthy Robert R. Church Sr. in 1885. (Memphis Room.)

13

Another important antebellum pioneer was Joseph Clouston (1814–1894). Born in Fayette County, Tennessee, Joseph worked as a barber, saving his earnings to purchase freedom for himself and his mother. He migrated to Memphis and became one of the first African Americans to own a business on Beale Street. City directories list him as the proprietor of a barbershop and grocery store by the 1860s, both located at 145 Beale Street. He served on the Memphis City Council in 1873, representing the Fifth Ward during Reconstruction. Clouston's enterprise made him a rich man: he amassed a fortune of over $100,000. He also owned three farms and more than 100 slaves. Joseph, his wife, Dora, and their three children lived in a large home across the street from Zion Cemetery on the road later known as South Parkway East. (Memphis Room.)

Dora Clouston is pictured here around the beginning of the 20th century. The photograph was taken by John Newton, the earliest known professional black photographer in Memphis. (Mississippi Valley Collection.)

Robert R. Church Sr. (1839–1912) was the South's first African American millionaire and one of the most successful black businessmen in the country. Born in Holly Springs, Mississippi, to a slave seamstress and a white riverboat captain, he made a fortune in real estate buying up downtown properties after the Civil War. When a devastating yellow fever epidemic reduced Memphis to a taxing district in 1878, Church was first to purchase a $1,000 bond to help restore the city charter. His diversified business enterprises included restaurants, hotels, and saloons. Church was skilled in buying and supplying establishments with fine food and liquor from years of training as a steward under his father on steamboat passages. Below, this saloon at Main and Gayoso Streets, which Church renamed the Bob Church Saloon, was one of his first investments after the Civil War. (Both, Mississippi Valley Collection.)

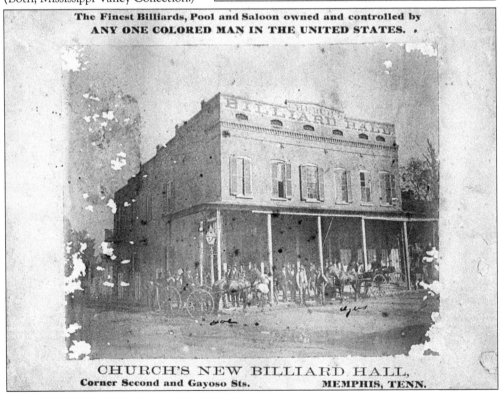

The Finest Billiards, Pool and Saloon owned and controlled by ANY ONE COLORED MAN IN THE UNITED STATES.

CHURCH'S NEW BILLIARD HALL,
Corner Second and Gayoso Sts.   MEMPHIS, TENN.

Church established the Solvent Savings Bank and Trust Company in 1906 on Beale Street. As president, Church oversaw the first black bank in Memphis as well as the third-largest African American bank in the country. Church and his partners, including Josiah Settle and Thomas Hayes, emphasized conservative banking practices of business expansion and moneymaking. The bank was the core of economic development for Beale Street and the black community. By 1912, deposits were in excess of $100,000. Church built Church's Park and Auditorium on Beale Street in 1899. He managed the facility, with its seating capacity of 2,200, as recreational space for black Memphians denied access to public parks. In 1900, Church was a delegate to the Republican National Convention. It was said of Robert Church Sr. that he was first, last, and always for Memphis. (Both, Mississippi Valley Collection.)

Josiah Settle (1850–1915) was a prominent attorney. He was born in East Tennessee to a slave named Nancy Graves and a wealthy white planter named Josiah Settle. Settle freed his common-law slave wife and all of their children, eventually moving the family to Ohio. Josiah entered Howard University and obtained his law degree in 1875. He moved to Sardis, Mississippi, where he practiced law for 10 years and was active in politics. In 1885, Settle migrated to Memphis to take up an appointed position as assistant attorney general of the Criminal Court of Shelby County. He returned to private practice after two years on the bench, having earned a reputation as a gifted lawyer and orator. In 1890, Settle married Fannie McCullough, director of music at Lemoyne Normal Institute. The Settles attended Emmanuel Episcopal Church and lived on South Orleans Street. Journalist and activist Ida B. Wells boarded with the Settles when she lived in Memphis. The photograph shows (from left to right) Josiah and Fannie Settle with Mary Church Terrell, Robert Church Sr., and Anna Wright Church. It was taken in Kentucky. (Memphis Room.)

Julia Hooks (1852–1942) was born in Lexington, Kentucky, to a former slave mother who had been manumitted at 16. A child prodigy, Julia enrolled in Berea College in 1869, where she also became the first African American to teach integrated classes in Kentucky. In 1876, Julia moved to Memphis and was soon appointed principal of the Virginia Avenue School. Dissatisfied with the quality of education for black children, she founded two private schools: the Hooks Cottage School for kindergarten and elementary school grades, and the integrated Hooks School of Music. Active in community service, Hooks was instrumental in the establishment of a juvenile detention home for black youth in 1902. Julia's husband, Charles Hooks, was killed by one of the wards, but she continued her ministry of youth and adult prisoners. Julia Hooks's compassion was why she became known to many in Memphis as the "Angel of Beale Street." In 1917, she became one of the charter members of the NAACP. Her grandson, Benjamin Hooks, was appointed its national executive director in 1977. (Mississippi Valley Collection.)

In 1891, Julia Hooks initiated the establishment of the Old Folks and Orphans Home on Old Hernando Road. The organization purchased 25 acres to build a home for elderly women and orphans in the black community. David Washington constructed the building, and Julia helped to pay off the mortgage by giving concerts. (Memphis Room.)

This composition book was used at Hooks Cottage School, the private kindergarten and elementary school located in Julia Hooks's home at 578 South Lauderdale Street. The small African American elite developing in Memphis often home-schooled their children and also sent them to Hooks Cottage School. *Around the World* belonged to Robert Church Jr., son of millionaire Robert Church Sr. (Mississippi Valley Collection.)

Martha Ferguson was one of the few early Memphians actually born in the city. She was a successful businesswoman in an era when commercial opportunities for women were rare. During the 1870s, she opened a hand laundry that specialized in the care of fragile fabrics like silk, lace, and linen. (Mississippi Valley Collection.)

Realizing the importance of education, Martha Ferguson enrolled her daughter, Ida, in Antioch College at Yellow Springs, Ohio, during the 1870s. Ida was therefore able to attend college with her friend Lucy Jane Wright. Ida was a schoolteacher before she married. She is pictured here with her husband, Lewis, (standing) and their three sons, (from left to right) Lemuel, Eugene, and William, and the family dogs. (Mississippi Valley Collection.)

Historic First Baptist Beale, at the corner of Beale and Fourth Streets, still proudly stands today as the first multistoried brick church in the South erected by former slaves to serve their own community. It was founded in 1863; the early congregation was poor and first met on the lot under trees. It took five years to complete the basement, and the cornerstone was not laid until 1871. Work stopped on the church in 1873 during the yellow fever epidemic. Sorrow visited the congregation again when their beloved pastor, Thomas Henderson, who was guiding them through their struggles, sacrifices, and hardships, died in 1877. First Baptist Church of Beale Street, as it was then known, was finally completed in 1878. Gen. Ulysses S. Grant was a guest speaker in 1880. (Both, Memphis Room.)

Following the Civil War, black Memphians organized a burial association called the United Sons and Daughters of Zion. They purchased 16 acres outside the city limits for use as a cemetery along South Parkway East. Active from 1873 until 1925, Zion, the oldest black cemetery in Memphis, contains the remains of almost 25,000 African Americans who lived and died between the late 19th and early 20th centuries. It is the burial place of three black merchants, Thomas Moss, William Stewart, and Calvin McDowell, 1892 lynching victims who ignited the anti-lynching crusade of Ida B. Wells. Zion's broad view of the human experience spans the Civil War, emancipation, Reconstruction, yellow fever epidemics, World War I, and the Jim Crow eras. Ignored for decades, it is now going through an extensive cleanup effort. Zion Cemetery is on the National Register of Historic Places. (Both, Memphis Room.)

The plots in Morris Henderson Circle are decorated with the most elaborate monuments. Located on a softly rising hill on the east side of Center Road, it contains the graves of Rev. Thomas Henderson, the beloved minister of First Baptist Beale, and his family. The area includes obelisks, curbed plots, and fenced-in spaces. Henderson's monument is decorated with a portrait sculpture of the deceased framed around the base with curling vines. Reverend Henderson looks up with a solemn, straightforward expression. One can only imagine the expense that was probably donated by the entire congregation in order to memorialize Reverend Henderson in this manner. (Both, Memphis Room.)

Bishop Charles H. Mason (1862–1961) founded the Church of God in Christ (COGIC). Mason was born into slavery near Bartlett, Tennessee. Sickly and haunted by visions as a child, Mason was healed in 1880 when, as he claimed, "the glory of God came down upon him." Bishop Mason organized the Church of God in Christ in 1897, establishing his congregation and headquarters in Memphis. They first worshipped in a building on South Wellington Street overlooking a bayou. After a flood forced the congregation to relocate, a lot was purchased at 672 South Lauderdale Street, and Temple Church of God in Christ was built in 1910. The church outgrew the boundaries of North America after the Home and Missionary Board was organized in 1925 by women in the congregation. Missionaries were sent to the West Indies in 1927 and West Africa in 1929. By 1935, there were over 20 COGIC churches in Memphis, prospering alongside the predominant Baptists, the 11 AME churches, and 17 CME congregations. Today the Church of God in Christ is the largest Pentecostal church in the United States. (Department of Art.)

The Right Reverend Edward Thomas Demby (1869–1957) was the leading figure in the desegregation of the Episcopal Church, holding the office of bishop from 1918 until 1934. Demby was ordained a deacon in 1898 and a priest in 1899 while working in the Diocese of Tennessee. In 1907, Demby served as rector of Emmanuel Church in Memphis. He was then appointed secretary of the segregated Southern convocations and the Archdeacon for Colored Work. While serving as archdeacon, Demby was elected the first African American bishop as Suffragan Bishop for Colored Work in the Diocese of Arkansas and the Province of the Southwest. In spite of the humiliation suffered from the white leadership, Demby was not dissuaded from his great work, bringing African Americans back to an institution they had abandoned after emancipation. He founded and edited the *Southwest Churchman* and wrote many devotional books. His story is most recently told by Michael Beary in *Black Bishop: Edward T. Demby and the Struggle for Racial Equality in the Episcopal Church*, published in 2001. (Mississippi Valley Collection.)

Lincoln Chapel School was one of the first private educational institutions for African American children in Memphis. It was built in 1866 by the American Missionary Association. The school was rebuilt after the race riot of 1866 with 150 students and 6 teachers. After Dr. Francis Lemoyne, a Northern abolitionist, donated $20,000 in 1870, it reopened in a new building at 284 Orleans Road and was renamed LeMoyne Normal and Commercial School. Its mission was to prepare young African American men and women to teach. Lemoyne awarded its first two teaching diplomas in 1876 and added a high school in 1901. Pictured below in the fourth row, seventh from the right is Anna Wright, one of those first two graduating students. (Both, Memphis Room.)

James P. Newton was the first professional black photographer in Memphis. City directories list Newton as the proprietor of his own photography studio on 134 South Main Street in the 1890s. Sources describe his work as of the highest quality and state that Newton's skills with a camera were widely known. He operated his studio until about 1909, when he may have relocated to Chicago, where he had extensive property interests. The few existing examples of Newton's work indicate that he was the preferred photographer of Memphis's black elite. The black stockings, shoes, and lacey jacket are typical dress for upper middle class children. The African American woman pictured below may be dressed in traditional mourning, wearing garments dyed black, including the veiled hat. (Both, Mississippi Valley Collection.)

By the end of the 19th century, Memphis was a segregated city, with blacks and whites separated by neighborhoods, churches, schools, cemeteries, and all public facilities and spaces, including hospitals, restaurants, hotels, and parks. It was reinforced in 1896 when the U.S. Supreme Court upheld segregation by sanctioning the practice of "separate but equal." Integrated social activities like the one depicted in this 1899 south Memphis neighborhood were increasingly prohibited. (Memphis Room.)

Lymus Wallace was one of the last African Americans to hold political office in Memphis. Wallace served two four-year terms as alderman in 1882 and 1886. He was the first black man elected to the office, which was essentially membership on the Board of Public Works. He was a member of the Board of Education at one time and was the last African American elected to the city council, serving from 1885 to 1891. One of his most effective responses to the needs of the black community occurred during the flood of 1897, when areas 100 miles north of the city and 200 miles south of Memphis were submerged. Thousands of refugees poured into the city. The local relief association at Front Street and Adams Avenue turned blacks away. Lymus Wallace organized a black relief agency that did as much as possible to aid black victims of the flood. The Wallaces lived about a block from their close friends, Robert and Anna Church Sr., in the 400 block of South Lauderdale Street. After Lymus's death, the Wallace family moved to Chicago. (Memphis Room.)

Beale Street was originally a melting pot of Germans, Italians, African Americans, Irish, and Jews. By the beginning of the 20th century, however, it was the epicenter of black politics, business, culture, and community in the Mid-South. This view dates to about 1915 and was taken looking east from Beale and Hernando Streets. The street is populated by black businessmen, patrons, and pedestrians. (Department of Art.)

Two

MEMPHIS RENAISSANCE
THE EARLY 20TH CENTURY

Beale Street was critical to the emergence of Memphis as an important crossroads of black urban culture at the beginning of the 20th century. It was the site of black Memphians' struggle to grasp the opportunities of a new age in spite of racial oppression, violence, and enforced segregation. It is said that three leaders contributed significantly to the growth and renown of Beale Street: Robert R. Church Sr. in business, Robert Church Jr. in politics, and W. C. Handy in music. Bob Church Jr., W. C. Handy, and George Washington "Lieutenant" Lee were most influential during the first half of the 20th century, continuing the legacy of economic development and race pride initiated by 19th-century pioneers. From left to right, Church, Handy, and Lee are gathered together in front of Bob Church's office at 392 Beale Street in this famous photograph. (Memphis Room.)

Robert R. Church Jr. was born in 1885. He attended Oberlin College and the Packard School of Business in New York. Returning to Memphis in 1907, he strategically built a career as the most influential African American leader in the Republican Party. In 1917, he founded the Memphis branch of the NAACP, which was the first NAACP branch in Tennessee and the South. He was a member of the NAACP National Board of Directors for many years. Opposed forcefully by white Republicans, Church was still a Memphis delegate to eight successive Republican conventions from 1912 to 1940. Robert Church Jr. affected the appointments of the U.S. Attorney for West Tennessee, two federal judges, and the postmasters for Memphis. Church was frequently at odds with democratic mayor E. H. "Boss" Crump. In 1940, the Crump machine destroyed Church's political base. He moved to Washington, D.C., and continued his long political career. Church was a member of the board of directors for a permanent fair employment practices committee, the Equal Employment Opportunity Commission (EEOC). He died in 1952 after campaigning for Dwight D. Eisenhower. (Mississippi Valley Collection.)

Church established and financed the Lincoln League, an organization of black Republicans, in 1916. The Lincoln League organized registration drives, paid poll taxes, and sponsored candidates. African American leaders met in New Orleans in 1918 to form the nationwide Lincoln League of America. This is a picture of the first Lincoln League meeting in 1916. (Mississippi Valley Collection.)

"The Gentleman from Memphis," as described by an editorial in the Pittsburg *Courier*, was known for his organizational abilities and his analytical mind. Keeping up-to-date demanded a regular reading schedule of politics throughout the country: daily newspapers like the Memphis dailies, the Chicago newspapers, the *New York Times*, and a diversity of black weekly papers. Signed portraits of national Republican leaders line Church's office walls. (Memphis Room.)

George Washington Lee (1894–1976) was one of the most important civic leaders in Memphis for almost 40 years. Promoted to an officer for bravery on the battlefield during World War I, he was widely known as "Lieutenant" Lee. In 1919, Robert Church Jr. persuaded Lee to return to Memphis and work as his assistant in the Republican Party. He was one of the founders of the National Negro Insurance Association and was active in the community as grand commissioner of the Improved Benevolent and Protective Order of Elks of the World. (Memphis Room.)

Lieutenant Lee was also an author, completing two novels and a collection of short stories. His first and most successful book was *Beale Street, Where the Blues Began* (1934). An alternate selection for the Book of the Month Club, it remains the best account of Beale Street in its early incarnation as legend and lore. His second novel was the colorful tale of a roustabout named River George. (Memphis Room.)

The 1910s also found black Memphians drawn into the Great War. Blair T. Hunt trained at Fort Meade, Maryland, and was ranked as a first lieutenant because of his college education. He was placed in the Chaplains Corps with the 340th Service Battalion and served in France. Hunt's portrait was taken at the Hooks Brothers photography studio on Beale Street. (Memphis Room.)

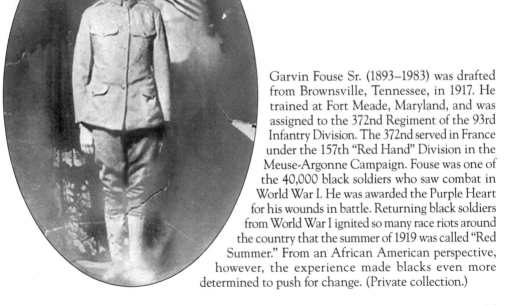

Garvin Fouse Sr. (1893–1983) was drafted from Brownsville, Tennessee, in 1917. He trained at Fort Meade, Maryland, and was assigned to the 372nd Regiment of the 93rd Infantry Division. The 372nd served in France under the 157th "Red Hand" Division in the Meuse-Argonne Campaign. Fouse was one of the 40,000 black soldiers who saw combat in World War I. He was awarded the Purple Heart for his wounds in battle. Returning black soldiers from World War I ignited so many race riots around the country that the summer of 1919 was called "Red Summer." From an African American perspective, however, the experience made blacks even more determined to push for change. (Private collection.)

The beginning of the 20th century saw increasing numbers of black Memphians establish their own businesses and acquire real estate. The new entrepreneurs were tailors, undertakers, grocers, caterers, blacksmiths, and so forth. The oldest African American business in Memphis remains T. H. Hayes and Sons Funeral Home. Thomas Hayes's family moved to Tennessee in 1880, settling on the Ames Plantation. He worked a variety of jobs while attending Howe Institute in Memphis. Hayes opened four grocery stores that all failed before the fifth store was successful. Hayes entered the undertaking business at 245 Poplar Avenue in 1902. His business was notable for the range of services he offered, affordable to the working class and the elite. The quality of service was excellent. Funerals were conducted with modern equipment, consisting of 12 horses from his stables, 10 rigs, 5 hearses, 1 ambulance, and landau carriages. In 1913, he purchased a large residence at 680 South Lauderdale Street and remodeled it to accommodate the funeral business on the first floor while the family lived above. He is pictured with his wife and sons. (Memphis Room.)

Lemuel Lewis (seated at right) also came from a family of entrepreneurs. His grandmother Martha Ferguson operated a laundry that specialized in the cleaning of fine linens, while his mother, Ida, worked as a schoolteacher before her marriage. Lemuel and his brother operated a tailoring shop. Lemuel had cards made to advertise his work featuring a photograph of himself wearing a suit of his own design and workmanship. (Right, Memphis Room; below, Mississippi Valley Collection.)

George Henderson established a black business college in Memphis in 1914. Henderson was known for his business acumen, emphasizing exceptional skills in typing and shorthand. Henderson Business College operated from a house at 590 St. Paul Avenue for many years until Henderson relocated it to 530 Linden Avenue in 1939. (Memphis Room.)

The facility was made up of three structures: the administration building, the graphic arts building, and a dormitory for young women. Modern equipment was used to teach courses in accounting, typing, and printing skills. Henderson Business College was recognized by the State Board of Education. The National Bureau of Office Proficiency Standards also commissioned Henderson to prepare students for administrative exams. (Memphis Room.)

Dr. J. E. Walker established Universal Life Insurance Company in Memphis in 1923. Born into poverty in Mississippi, he completed medical school and opened a small medical practice in Indianola, Mississippi, delivering babies. However, he was more interested in banks and insurance, helping to organize Mississippi Life Insurance Company in 1909. When the company moved to Memphis, Walker resigned and founded Universal Life. As the company grew, it moved from a small wood building that housed the Fraternal Bank to a two-story brick structure on Hernando and Beale Streets in 1926. (Mississippi Valley Collection.)

Robert Lewis built the first black baseball park in the country at the corner of Crump Boulevard and South Lauderdale Street in the early 1920s. Lewis then organized the city's first black baseball team to play in it, the Memphis Red Sox. Members of the old Negro American League, the Memphis Red Sox played against other black teams when baseball was America's favorite pastime. Wonderful baseball games took place in Lewis Park before large, well-dressed, enthusiastic crowds. It was also a public service space for black Memphians, who played football games, held track meets, and organized rallies in its facilities. Lewis sold the Memphis Red Sox and Lewis Park to Dr. William Martin and his brothers in 1927. They renamed it Martin Stadium. The structure was razed in the 1960s, but the family business, R. S. Lewis and Sons Funeral Home at 374 Vance Avenue, is still in business. The photograph pictures the Memphis Red Sox at Martin Stadium in 1934. (Department of Art.)

William Martin was the oldest of the four
Martin brothers, early-20th-century pioneers
in medicine, sports, and business. They were
born in Senatobia, Mississippi. Their parents
moved to Memphis and sent the brothers
to Lemoyne Normal Institute and Meharry
Medical School in Nashville, Tennessee.
Martin established his medical practice
in Memphis in 1907. (Memphis Room.)

J. B. Martin was a pharmacist. He founded the South Memphis Drug Store at 907 Florida Avenue
in 1910. He was a prominent Republican leader. "Boss" Crump forced him out of town in 1940
by ordering police to harass his customers. Martin moved to Chicago and recreated his career in
sports and business. J. B. and his brothers were principal owners of the Memphis Red Sox. Martin is
standing to the left with other owners of the team in front of his drugstore. (Memphis Room.)

Memphis physicians like the Martin brothers were prohibited from practicing in public or private hospitals, so they had to be resourceful in establishing separate health care facilities for blacks. Dr. Miles Lynk founded the University of West Tennessee in Jackson, Tennessee, in 1900 to train and educate medical professionals. Dr. Lynk moved the school to 1190 South Phillips Place in Memphis in 1907. By the time the school closed about 1930, most of the early black health professionals in Memphis had received training in medicine, nursing, dentistry, and pharmacy. Dr. Francis M. Kneeland, one of the city's pioneer women physicians, was a faculty member and the director of nursing. The school attracted students from all over the United States and six foreign countries. There are several students from Japan pictured in the graduating class of 1923. Dr. Lynk was also an author. His best-known publications were *The Black Troopers or the Daring Deeds, of the Negro Soldier in the Spanish American War* (1899) and *Sixty Years of Medicine or the Life and Times of Dr. Miles V. Lynk, An Autobiography* (1951). (Memphis Room.)

Dr. Cleveland A. Terrell and his nephew, Dr. L. O. Patterson, were cofounders of Terrell-Patterson Infirmary at 159 Beale Street. Terrell was a graduate of Meharry Medical College in Nashville. During the 1910s, they established Jane Terrell Memorial Hospital at 698 Williams Street. The new hospital featured a training school for nurses, and several of the graduates are pictured here. (Department of Art.)

COLLINS CHAPEL HOME AND HOSPITAL
418 ASHLAND COURT, MEMPHIS, TENN.

is Hospital is equipped with every latest appliance invented to serve surgical skill. Additional instruments of great e recently been selected and installed under the personal direction of the Surgeon-in-Chief.
ted in the largest and most thriving settlement of colored people in the South. Memphis is the natural capital of mo Negroes.
uilding is a modern structure designed, erected and fitted for the use of Collins Hospital, and nothing else. Its locatio city from a striking eminence, and every convenience is at hand. Three hundred cases, running the list of diseases, ha eight months. The doors are open to the patients of every colored practitioner of standing.
NING SCHOOL—A Training School for Nurses is established in connection with the hospital, and affords a fine opportu ining a sound course a nurse training

Collins Chapel Hospital was another critical facility that offered health care to African Americans in Memphis and surrounding areas. This advertisement for the hospital, dated 1915, appeared in a black political paper started by Roscoe Simmons. The hospital featured a maternity ward, an operating room, a sterilizing room, and a correctional ward. Dr. J. B. Martin became superintendent of Collins Chapel Hospital in 1920 and was named staff president in 1955. (Mississippi Valley Collection.)

While African Americans made advances as entrepreneurs, many more worked in the service industries. Alonzo Locke (center) was one of the most experienced headwaiters in the hotel industry. His career began at the Gayoso Hotel in 1906. In 1925, he was promoted to headwaiter of the grand Peabody Hotel. Locke served many celebrities and was famous for his ability to remember names. When Memphians travelled to Europe, foreigners who had dined at the world famous Peabody inquired about Alonzo Locke. Locke trained generations of young black men in the finer skills of efficiency, attention to detail, courtesy, and self-esteem required in the business of satisfying elite clientele, a profession now called hotel management. He helped to organize the Hotelmen's Improvement Club in 1924, and his influence was such that he helped maintain positions in the Memphis hotel system for black men during the Depression when white workers took over a number of jobs formerly held by blacks. When Locke died in 1947, more than 1,000 people attended his funeral. Alonzo Locke Elementary School is named in his honor. (Memphis Room.)

Three

LEGACY
THE HOOKS BROTHERS OF MEMPHIS

The Hooks brothers founded the second-oldest business in Memphis, opening a photography studio at 162 Beale Street in 1907. They remained active in the photography business until the 1970s, capturing a visual record of black Memphians' cultural and social history that is unmatched. The sons of Charles and Julia Hooks, they lived near prosperous family friends like the Churches on Lauderdale Street; hence much of their early work documented not only early history, but specifically the small black elite and upper class developing around the beginning of the 20th century. Henry (left) and Robert are seen in an early image developed from glass-plate negatives. (Department of Art.)

The Hooks brothers took this baby picture of Thelma Estelle Murphy. She was born in Memphis on April 23, 1914. Charlie Clifford, Thelma's father, moved his family to Chicago when she was about two years old. He migrated farther north for better job opportunities. He got a job with the postal service and moved to the Westside to a small apartment on Calumet Street. Thelma and her sister, Verna, returned to Memphis to spend summers with their grandmother Etta Murphy, helping her to run a small general store. Below, the photograph of grandmother Murphy with her son Charlie was taken in Memphis during one of the return trips home; the photographer is unknown. (Both, Diane Wright Collection.)

The Hooks brothers took many pictures of the Church family, given their importance at the pinnacle of the African American elite. The early years of Robert Church Sr.'s granddaughter Roberta Church are well documented by the photographers, including pictures as a toddler, young girl, and young adult. Roberta's kindergarten picture, taken in 1922, depicts the children she attended school with in grades one through four. Helen Wheeler, the teacher on the left, was from Massachusetts. A Miss Talon stands on the right. Roberta stands next to Wheeler and is wearing a large dark bow in her hair. The Hooks brothers took this Christmas photograph (below) inside of the Church home. It showcases the dolls and other toys Roberta received and dates to about 1927. (Both, Mississippi Valley Collection.)

The Church family had connections all over the country. Many of their friends were celebrities. The Hooks photographed the famous when they visited Memphis, including bluesman Robert Johnson. They reportedly photographed Booker T. Washington when he visited the Churches and gave a speech in Memphis. Unfortunately, this glass-plate negative was lost in a fire in the 1970s that destroyed some of the collection. Pictured here are Annette Church (right in both), sister of Robert Jr., and her friend, Helen Chestnut. Helen was the daughter of the noted African American author Charles Chestnut. When she visited Annette in 1914, they had pictures taken at the Hooks Brothers studio on Beale Street. They even dressed alike. (Both, Mississippi Valley Collection.)

These two images are not Hooks Brothers photographs. They are, however, examples of class and social status as it relates to the black elite in Memphis at the beginning of the 20th century. Both photographs were sent to the Churches and were treasured items in the family's photograph collection. Robert Church Jr. was a close friend of the famous African American comedian and vaudeville performer Bert Williams (pictured at right), whose career began with the Ziegfeld Follies. The well-dressed gentleman pictured below is James Weldon Johnson, author of the "Negro National Anthem," "Lift every Voice and Sing." (Both, Mississippi Valley Collection.)

Many family friends and neighbors who also lived on Lauderdale Street or nearby were photographed by the Hooks brothers, and these images are preserved in the Church family collection. The Churches were close friends with Charles and Carrie Bowles. Charles Bowles was a blacksmith. Their daughter Nellie appears in a number of photographs from childhood to young adult. They were well educated, well mannered, well dressed, and cultivated. These attributes of an upper-class lifestyle are much in evidence in these two photographs of Nellie Bowles in a fashionable coat and dress and at a music or literary recital of some type. Attendance at such fine-art activities was common and was even described in certain social settings in Memphis in the diaries kept by Ida B. Wells. (Left, Mississippi Valley Collection; below, Memphis Room.)

Early on, the Hooks brothers showed an interest in photographing African American women. They experimented with different lighting techniques that best complimented the diversity in African American skin tones and features. They also carefully chose backdrops and settings, as well as positions and group arrangements, to show the sitter off to her best advantage. This portrait of Roberta Church is a beautiful example. Roberta Church had a long career in public service following the death of her father in 1952. She became the first African American woman elected to public office in Memphis and Shelby County. When she was appointed to the U.S. Department of Labor as a minority groups consultant in 1953, she became the highest-ranking black woman in federal government. After returning to Memphis in the 1980s, she pursued research, writing, and community service. She coauthored *The Robert R. Churches of Memphis* with her aunt, Annette Church, in 1974. (Mississippi Valley Collection.)

The Hooks brothers documented all aspects of African American life in Memphis. Many of their images captured physical spaces—places, buildings, and streets—that have changed or been demolished and exist no longer except in a Hooks Brothers photograph. The picture above shows a craftsman-style dwelling and a black woman, probably a member of the family, sitting on the porch. The picture below is of Jackson's Drugstore at 321 Beale Street in 1915. G. R. Jackson was one of the first black pharmacists in Memphis. (Above, Mississippi Valley Collection; below, Department of Art.)

Christopher Roulhac was a medical examiner in Memphis for over 50 years. He taught on the faculty of the University of West Tennessee Medical College. His daughter, Alma Roulhac Booth (below, first row center), was active in Links Inc., a social organization that supported the goals and aspirations of black women. The Roulhacs lived at 810 East McLemore Avenue in a house that was built in 1914, the same year Alma was born. Dr. Roulhac purchased the home in 1926 when black professionals moving into the area changed the neighborhood from all-white to racially mixed. Today the home is one of the rare black private homes individually listed on the National Register of Historic Places. It is a within walking distance of the Stax Museum and has been turned into a bed-and-breakfast. Both photographs were taken by the Hooks brothers. (Right, Memphis Room; below, private collection.)

This photograph of the Pullman car porters was taken in the 1910s by the Hooks brothers. The Brotherhood of Sleeping Car Porters and Maids was a labor union organized in 1925. A. Philip Randolph was the president. The Pullman Company hired blacks as porters, and it was a sought-after position. In spite of the service and menial aspects of the job, its salary and benefits were better than most work open to black Americans. (Department of Art.)

Four

MEMPHIS
THE MUSICAL CITY IS BORN

The black musical heritage of America was largely preserved through the work of bandleaders and orchestras. They popularized the original sounds of the field hands, roustabouts, and railroad section hands who sang as they worked. Delta laborers travelled up the Mississippi River to enjoy the saloons and bawdyhouses on Beale Street, where their songs were heard by bandleaders and composers in Memphis, who set the new sounds to music with urban, jazz influences. W. C. Handy was born in Alabama and studied music at the Florence District School. He toured the United States, Mexico, Cuba, and the Mississippi Delta in 1896, where he first heard work songs and field hollers. In Memphis in 1909, he incorporated the material into a selection called "Mr. Crump." The song was published as the "Memphis Blues" in 1912. Handy wrote his best music on Beale Street, including "Beale Street Blues" and "St. Louis Blues." Even after Handy and his business partner, Harry Pace, moved to New York and established a successful publishing company, he often returned to visit his favorite city and friends. (Department of Art.)

John Love was one of the city's most brilliant bandleaders. An expert musician on the cornet, he was a pupil of the great Matt Reynolds, bandleader in an army unit during the Civil War. Love became a music teacher and orchestra leader, teaching more men music in his half-century career in Memphis than any other instructor. In the 1870s and 1880s, Love instructed early players by ear, developing his pupils' ear for music so acutely that one needed only to hear the bandleader strike a chord and he could fill in. The known bands Love developed include the Chickasaw Band, the Young Men's Band, and the Letter Carrier's Band, the most outstanding. All of the members were mail carriers with the post office except for his wife, Annabelle, who was an expert on the flute and also performed with the group. The Letter Carrier's Band entertained at every public gathering in Memphis and travelled throughout the United States, Mexico, and Canada. The band is pictured during the 1920s with John Love kneeling on the left. (Memphis Room.)

Blues made Beale Street and Memphis famous as an entertainment district where African Americans readily found employment as entertainers on the Vaudeville circuit. This photograph depicts two performers at the Palace Theater in the 1920s. The Palace was the largest theater for blacks in the South. It was built by Fred Barrasso and the Pacini brothers. Church Auditorium and the Grand Theater were the other two important sites for black theatrical talent on Beale Street. Showman Fred Barrasso organized the first circuit in the United States to employ African American entertainers in 1907. His brother, A. Barrasso, helped to organize the Theater Owners Bookers Association (TOBA) circuit in 1909, which committed to hiring black entertainers in 40 performance sites across the United States. The organizations encouraged investment in the building of black theaters and the demand for black professionals in the entertainment business. These factors were critical in the development of Memphis as a significant site for black musical entertainment centered on Beale Street. (Department of Art.)

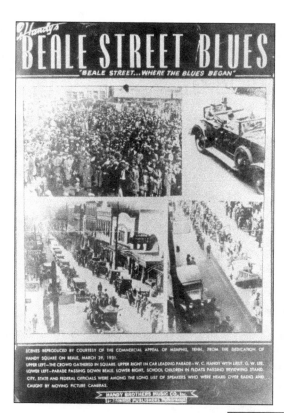

SCENES REPRODUCED BY COURTESY OF THE COMMERCIAL APPEAL OF MEMPHIS, TENN., FROM THE DEDICATION OF HANDY SQUARE ON BEALE, MARCH 29, 1931.
UPPER LEFT—THE CROWD GATHERED IN SQUARE. UPPER RIGHT IN CAR LEADING PARADE—W. C. HANDY WITH LIEUT. G. W. LEE. LOWER LEFT—PARADE PASSING DOWN BEALE. LOWER RIGHT, SCHOOL CHILDREN IN FLOATS PASSING REVIEWING STAND. CITY, STATE AND FEDERAL OFFICIALS WERE AMONG THE LONG LIST OF SPEAKERS WHO WERE HEARD OVER RADIO AND CAUGHT BY MOVING PICTURE CAMERAS.

As a result, Beale Street emerged as a significant public site for African American celebration in Memphis and the wider Mid-South. Beale Street became a symbol of freedom for the new black communities. The early-20th-century black communities that developed following emancipation, Reconstruction, and migration from rural areas were diverse, complex, and, above all, urban. In cities like Memphis, the early concentration of blacks around the Beale Street area allowed them to gather together and mobilize in large, highly visible ways. Public spaces of freedom like Beale Street offered blacks protection, allowed their institutions to thrive, and reinforced a common racial identity. No wonder black Memphians frequently celebrated events with music, performance, and a public parade down Beale Street. (Both, Memphis Room.)

The influence of Beale Street, Memphis, and its black musical heritage inspired a rare opportunity to work in the early film industry for African American actors. In 1928, Hollywood director King Vidor chose Memphis and Arkansas as location sites for his movie *Hallelujah!* Released in 1929, Vidor's film was significant as the first black musical and the first sound film to use an all-black cast. Several Memphians were cast in the film, including Georgia Woodruff, Robert Couch, and Milton Dickerson, and many participated as extras. King Vidor hired well-known choral director Eva Jessye as music supervisor on the film. When one of the sopranos refused to travel south, Jessye asked a local train porter for advice. He suggested Georgia Woodruff, the singer and pianist at Metropolitan Baptist Church and Central Baptist Church under the direction of gospel songwriting pioneer Lucie B. Campbell. Georgia, then 22 years old, accompanied Jessye to the old Travellers Hotel on Vance Avenue near Fourth Street, where she auditioned and was hired. This movie still features the main actors, Nina Mae McKinney as Chick and Daniel Hayes as Zeke. (Memphis Room.)

Woodruff grew up in North Memphis and attended Grant Elementary School, Kortrecht High School, and Lemoyne Normal School. She had only been married to William Oscar Woodruff, who worked with the Illinois Central Railroad, for a year when she was hired as lead soprano in *Hallelujah!* When location shooting was over, Woodruff accompanied the cast to Hollywood to film the interior shots and record the soundtrack. She stayed in the Somerville Hotel with the other Dixie Jubilee Singers and actors. After *Hallelujah!*, Woodruff worked on the film *Babes of Dixie* in 1930 and completed a concert tour with the Dixie Jubilee Singers in New York. Afterwards her career ended, as she chose marriage and motherhood over the entertainment industry. (Both, Memphis Room.)

HOTEL SOMERVILLE   LOBBY

The parade, Zeke's preaching scene, and an effective baptizing scene were all filmed around what is now called Lenow Street. This movie still is the parade scene as it was filmed along Lenow Street. In 1928, an old bayou ran through the area and was used in the baptizing scene. The bayou was later filled in and was replaced by the Lemoyne Gardens housing project. Numerous Memphis extras worked in these scenes. (Memphis Room.)

Memphis extras Robert Couch and Milton Dickerson were discovered by the film crew dancing in the Peabody Hotel for pennies. Their dance routine was incorporated into the film. Robert was Rufus Thomas's partner when they performed as "Rufus and Bones" on the vaudeville circuit in the 1930s. They are pictured here with another child actor; from left to right are Milton Dickerson, Walter Tait, King Vidor, and Robert "Bones" Couch. Couch also worked in the Our Gang comedies. (Memphis Room.)

Hallelujah! is a landmark in sound film. In spite of stereotypes, it was the first Hollywood film to feature the black family. King Vidor shot on location in the South (King Vidor is pictured with his film crew above) because he viewed the region as the birthplace of African American culture. The film is strong in its depiction of black family life and community rituals like weddings, prayer, and celebrations. It is likewise rich in the presentation of different black music and dance forms, including spirituals, blues, work, and popular songs. Memphis, an early black urban center defined by its rich musical heritage, was the classic prototype for this film. It is fitting that one of Memphis's own, Georgia Woodruff (below, second row, left), contributed her art and left her city a rare visual legacy of a film now regarded as an American classic. (Both, Memphis Room.)

Five

EDUCATION
A STRUGGLE TO LEARN

By 1908, when prominent black educator G. P. Hamilton published *The Bright Side of Memphis*, he applauded the city's "eight large ward schools and one high school." Memphis now employed black principals and teachers educated in its school system. The schools were Greenwood, Kortrecht Grammar School, Grant, Carnes, Virginia Avenue, LaRose, Porter, Klondike, and Kortrecht High School. Private schools were Lemoyne Normal Institute, Julia Hooks Cottage School, Julia Hooks School of Music, and Howe Institute. Greenwood Colored Mission, established by the Methodist Episcopal Church South in 1862, founded Greenwood School in 1866 near Heistan Place and South Bellevue Boulevard. In 1899, Greenwood became a public school with two teachers instructing 198 pupils. In 1909, the school board constructed a new two-story, eight-room structure at 993 Melrose Street. Today old Greenwood School is G. P. Hamilton elementary, middle, and high schools. This is the eighth-grade graduation class of 1937 with principal J. W. Bailey. Greenwood CME Church took its name after the old Greenwood school because it allowed the congregation to meet there before they erected their first church in 1920. (Private collection.)

BOOKER T. WASHINGTON HIGH SCHOOL - COLORED

Kortrecht School originated as Clay Street School in 1874 at Clay and Fourth Streets. Black citizens succeeded in staffing the entire school with black teachers. Soon it became Kortrecht Grammar School, and it became Kortrecht High School in 1891. Green P. Hamilton was appointed principal of Kortrecht in 1892. He organized the first African American high school band in Memphis at Kortrecht about 1900. His most well-known music pupil was William Bailey, an expert saxophone and clarinet player who went on to play with Noble Sissle, Duke Ellington, and Fletcher Henderson. When Kortrecht became Booker T. Washington High School, the first high school built for blacks by the public school system, in 1926, G. P. Hamilton was appointed the first principal. Hamilton was also one of the first African American historians in Memphis, writing three books that are still critical references on the history of black Memphians: *The Bright Side of Memphis* (1908), *Beacon Lights of the Race* (1911), and a history of Booker T. Washington High School. Hamilton Elementary, Middle, and High Schools are named in his honor. (Memphis Room.)

Lawyer Brown (1871–1947) and Blair T. Hunt were two of the most respected educators in Memphis. Brown was known for his ability to relate to students. He attended Lemoyne Normal Institute and graduated from Fisk University. Brown was principal at LaRose, Greenwood, and Kortrecht High before his long career at Porter School. Brown Park and Playground on Orleans Street is named in his honor. Blair T. Hunt (1888–1978) also attended Lemoyne Normal Institute. He graduated from Morehouse College and received an Associate of Arts degree from Harvard University and a Master of Arts degree from Tennessee State Agricultural and Industrial State College (now Tennessee State University). He taught and was a principal at Porter, LaRose, and Kortrecht schools before he became principal of Booker T. Washington High School in 1932. Below, the school portrait of Hunt with students may be at Kortrecht Intermediate School, where he was appointed principal in 1926. (Both, Memphis Room.)

Howe Institute was established in 1888. Rev. Thomas Oscar Fuller, a prominent author and a church and civic leader, was principal between 1902 and 1929. Fuller attracted students, constructed buildings, and improved the curriculum by including classical studies in Greek and Latin. This was publicized so as not to offend white patrons. Fuller limited industrial training to printing and cooking classes. Howe Institute was one of the few schools in Memphis that offered black children an education above grammar school. Notable African Americans who attended Howe Institute included A. Langston Taylor, founder of Phi Beta Sigma Fraternity, Inc.; Dr. Hugh Gloster, a president of Morehouse College; and author Richard Wright from 1915 to 1916. Pictured here is the Clara Howe Building, constructed in 1909 as a dormitory for young black girls. Reverend Fuller was also the author of an acclaimed history book entitled *Pictorial History of the American Negro* in 1933. (Memphis Room.)

MANASSAS ELEMENTARY AND HIGH SCHOOL - COLORED

Manassas Street School began as an elementary school in Shelby County about 1900. Rosenwald funds helped Manassas acquire a library, science laboratories, and machinery for a home economics department. Manassas initiated the first sports program among black schools in Memphis in 1924, including football, basketball, and baseball. By the time Manassas graduated its first high school class in 1924, it was one of the largest Rosenwald schools in the world. Manassas became a city school in 1930. (Memphis Room.)

J. H. Hayes arrived at Manassas High School in 1929. During the Depression, he spent much time and money feeding, clothing, and sheltering students in the north Memphis community. He wrote many letters of reference for black men seeking employment at the local Firestone plant. He oversaw the reconstruction of Manassas between 1934 and 1938 when old wooden buildings became a modern brick school. Hayes's motto was "The Best is None too Good for Manassas." (Memphis Room.)

In 1901, Lemoyne Normal Institute moved to its present site on Walker Avenue. The first structure erected was Steele Hall, now on the National Register of Historic Places. The white faculty was integrated in 1910. Between 1924 and 1930, the school became a junior college. Harvard graduate Dr. Frank Sweeney became the first president in 1929 with a vision to transform Lemoyne into a college by building up football and debating. It worked. (Memphis Room.)

The football team became a member of the Southern Intercollegiate Athletic Conference, and Lemoyne participated in the first interracial debate in the South in 1931. It was the first black team to debate in the Midwest Debate Tournament in Iowa. In 1932, Lemoyne Junior College was chartered as a four-year institution. Changing its name to Lemoyne College, it was accredited its first A rating in 1939. This photograph, taken in front of Steele Hall, depicts one of the last junior classes to graduate from Lemoyne. (Pink Palace Museum.)

Six

WAR, RACE, AND CIVIL RIGHTS
THE 1940S AND 1950S

The 1940s and 1950s brought great changes to Memphis. Segregation was as its height when the Japanese attacked Pearl Harbor in December 1941. Racism did not stop black Americans from enlisting or from being drafted into service during World War II. The demands of war created new employment opportunities. Expectations were particularly high for black Memphians. In 1940, they had just gone through a police harassment campaign called the "Reign of Terror" that targeted black neighborhoods and businesses, the thousands of migrants still coming to the city, and African American leaders who publicly criticized the Crump machine. The struggle over race and rights in Memphis persisted with vigor during the war. Wartime prosperity and a growing black population made African Americans in Memphis determined to take part in the nation's rapid economic growth. This photograph shows three young sailors standing next to a recruiting sign in downtown Memphis. Note that the face in the sign has been darkened, possibly to encourage African Americans to enlist. (Department of Art.)

More than 500,000 African Americans served overseas during World War II. Most young black men from Memphis and surrounding rural communities had never been far from their hometowns, let alone overseas. Earnest Jenkins (pictured at left) was drafted from Hernando, Mississippi. He trained at Fort Benning, learning to parachute out of airplanes with the 101st Airborne Division, and ended up serving in the South Pacific. Jesse Sinclair (pictured below) was assigned to the 758th Tank Battalion and served in the European theater of operations. Black men were eligible for equal benefits provided by the government for those who served their country during World War II. The GI Bill transformed America. It allowed returning veterans to buy homes with little or no down payment or use the technical skills learned in their military training to get a job, including government positions. They could also start a business, attend high school or college, learn a trade, and qualify for medical care. (Private collections.)

The city constructed Kennedy General Hospital in 1942. Covering 160 acres at what are now Park Avenue and Getwell Road, it had 4,600 beds. Forty-four thousand soldiers were treated at Kennedy by the end of the war. It was also an important source of employment in the non-agricultural sector for black men and women during the war. Afterwards, it became the Veterans Administration Hospital. After the VA hospital relocated to Jefferson, Kennedy was acquired by the University of Memphis. The navy built the largest inland naval base in the country at Millington, Tennessee. The buildings included the Naval Hospital, the Naval Air Station, and the Naval Air Technical Training Center. Millington was a popular site for parties during the war. (Both, private collection.)

During the war, Memphis industries benefitted from lucrative government contracts like Plough, Inc.; National Fireworks; Fisher Body; Firestone; Kimberly-Clark; Quaker Oats; Kennedy General Hospital; and the new army and navy depots. White migrants were hired for better paying positions while black migrants were downgraded to service jobs and unskilled labor. Black laborers, like the men collecting scrap iron for the Loeberg Company in 1943 (above), helped fuel the union movement in Memphis, supported by thousands of black laborers at woodworking plants, cottonseed oil mills, cotton compresses, and lumber mills. Between 1941 and 1945, over 20,000 Memphis workers joined the Congress of Industrial Organizations (CIO). Black men working inside of plants were frequently classified as "helpers" or "aids" or restricted to the less technical and "intelligent" work, such as packing. Racist hiring practices that replaced them with less-qualified white women also forced black men to confront discrimination in the workplace. (Both, Memphis Room.)

African American women had their own problems with "Rosie the Riveter" as they struggled to escape domestic service. Work outside of private homes still found them in service, frequently as laundresses in low-wage, low-skill jobs like operating the presses. They worked in conditions that were hot, steamy, and unsanitary. In Memphis alone, there were 3,000 laundry workers, women and men, at places like Kraus Cleaners, Model-Laundry Cleaners, and Loeb's Laundry, when they struck for union recognition between 1941 and 1945. Black women also had to protect themselves against the sexual abuse of white male employers. Such grievances were filed by black women laundry workers at the Veterans Hospital and Kennedy General Hospital. By the end of the war, the workplace was not perfect, but black women gained higher wages, union representation, and respect for themselves as American workers. (Both, Memphis Room.)

After the war, discrimination in the workplace was not eliminated, but African Americans had some success getting hired in jobs that had previously excluded them. Above, black women workers pack bottles in the local Coca-Cola plant. The photograph below pictures black women and men working under a white supervisor at the same plant. Although Memphis remained segregated after World War II, the war directly influenced the march toward racial equality. (Both, Memphis Room.)

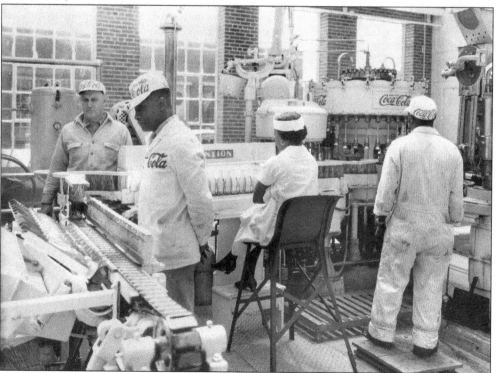

The city hired nine black police officers in 1948. This occurred in response to the demands of black Memphians who argued that this would reduce police brutality against African Americans. Black policemen in uniform walked foot patrols in black areas and could not arrest whites. Pictured here are some members of the original nine with additional recruits appointed in 1951. (Department of Art.)

Second Congregational Church honored some of the police officers with distinguished service awards. The Men's Fellowship at the church awarded three black lieutenants for good records as citizens as well as police officers. F. M. Campbell, principal of Melrose High School, is pictured making the awards. From left to right are Campbell, Lt. Thomas Marshall, Lt. Wendell Robinson, A. A. Latting (chairman of the awards committee), and Lt. R. J. Turner. (Mississippi Valley Collection.)

Only five years after the conclusion of World War II, the U.S. military was sent to battle on the Korean Peninsula. By the cease-fire in 1953, the war had done little to change the political balance of power between North and South Korea. However, the Korean War expedited the desegregation of the U.S. military. It was the most integrated institution in America by 1953. George Anderson Fouse served with the 5552nd MP Corps on Koje-do Island at the United Nations POW camp, where more than 170,000 communist and non-communist prisoners of war were held from 1950 to 1952. (Private collection.)

Seven

It's Rhythm and Blues
Black Popular Culture

By the 1940s, black musicians were popularizing jazz, blues, big band, swing, and bebop. Blacks were listening to rhythm and blues, a combination of blues and jazz-based styles. Musicians became famous by cutting records. African American talent depended on small independent record labels like Chess Records in Chicago or Duke and Son of Memphis. Such was the context in which Rufus Thomas (1917–2001) made his mark on the Memphis sound. Rufus started performing in the 1930s with vaudeville shows like the Rabbit Foot Minstrels. During the 1940s, Thomas hosted talent shows at the Palace Theater and was a deejay on WDIA Radio. His first national hit was "Bear Cat," recorded in 1953 at Sam Phillips's Memphis Recording Studio (later Sun Records). Thomas moved on to Stax Records, where he had five hits, including, "Walking the Dog," and "Do the Funky Chicken." Thomas punctuated his dynamic performance style with fashionable or flamboyant outfits. Rufus Thomas has been honored all over the world. A park is named after him in Poretta, Italy, home of the annual Sweet Soul Music Festival. (Department of Art.)

Entertainment like the Midnight Rambles is an example of how music crossed cultural boundaries, even within segregated Memphis. Beale Street's Midnight Rambles put on an all-black show for white-only patrons on Thursday nights. Entertainers like Rufus Thomas frequently performed to all-white audiences in Memphis nightclubs. The Brownskin Models were one of the most popular attractions on Beale Street: they drew large black and white crowds. (Mississippi Valley Collection.)

WDIA pioneered in the hiring of women deejays. In 1949, Willa Monroe started a show called "Tan Town Homemakers" targeting black middle-class housewives. The show was widely listened to by black women in the tri-state area. Monroe played music by singers like Sarah Vaughn, distributed advice, discussed recipes and society news, and interviewed prominent black women. The success of the daily format encouraged the hiring of other female deejays who brought their own talents to WDIA. Martha Jean Steinberg was known for her intelligent, sexy persona that introduced the latest R&B recordings. She moved to Detroit where she had a long career as "Martha Jean the Queen" and ended up purchasing her own radio station. Carlotta Stewart Watson, pictured above, was known as "Miss Carrie." She was popular as a motherly type who dispensed much needed advice with wisdom, wit, and laughter. (Mississippi Valley Collection.)

Herbert Brewster (1897–1987), a prominent Baptist minister, was one of the three "architects" of gospel music. He attended Howe Institute, then graduated from Roger Williams College. He became pastor of Pilgrim Baptist Church in 1925 and East Trigg Church in 1930, ministering at both churches for more than 50 years. He founded the Brewster Theological Seminary, which branched out into 25 cities. Brewster's songwriting talents were extraordinary. He wrote over 200 gospel songs, including "Lord I Tried" and "Move on up a Little Higher," recorded by Mahalia Jackson. Every Sunday he directed the "Gospel Treasure Hour" on WDIA. In 1941, he composed the fabulous religious drama *From Auction Block to Glory*. Performed in 1958 to encourage African Americans to register to vote, the cast required several hundred actors and a 1,000-member chorus. Brewster was honored by the Smithsonian Institution in 1987. Below is a 1935 picture of Reverend Brewster (center) with his East Trigg congregation. (Above, Department of Art; below, private collection.)

Theo Wade was an important promoter of gospel music in Memphis. He was born in Palestine, Arkansas, in 1906. His career began as a gospel vocalist with the famed Spirit of Memphis Quartet in the 1930s. He made the transition to gospel deejay in 1954. He was known for his good humor, jokes, and salesmanship, earning the nickname "Brother Theo Bless My Bones Wade" because this is what he would exclaim during breaks. He was a widely admired manager of gospel musicians, booking into Memphis churches such notables as the Soul Stirrers, the Dixie Hummingbirds, the Swan Silvertones, and Sam Cooke. During Theo Wade's career in the 1950s, black male quartets were the most popular gospel singers of the day. (Right, Mississippi Valley Collection; below, private collection.)

Maurice Hulbert Sr. was one of the best-loved personalities in the history of black Memphis. Maurice "Fess" Hulbert was an elegant dancer and opened the first black dancing studio in Memphis. His music combo was known as Hulbert's Low Down Hounds. Hulbert operated several restaurants, such as the Harlem House, the Flamingo, and the Manhattan. With his connections in business entertainment, Hulbert booked celebrities like Duke Ellington, Ethel Waters, and black baseball teams. He supported many community projects, founding the Robert R. Elks Lodge No. 1477, and always helped the Elks with their yearly Christmas Drive (pictured below). In the 1950s, Hulbert sponsored Blues Bowl Games, raising scholarships for black students. He is pictured at left in 1951 at the 14th Annual Blues Bowl game, when he was crowned king and Jana Cox queen, and they were honored with the presence of the great W. C. Handy. (Left, Mississippi Valley Collection; below, Memphis Room.)

Post–World War II nightclubs and restaurants were a critical part of promoting black music and social culture in Memphis. Tony's Inn, the Gay Hawk, Peggy's Patio, Club Flamingo, the Tropicana, Mitchell Hotel, the Hippodrome, and the Lumpkin Hotel were among the popular sites where Africans Americans gathered socially to dine and listen to the best local bands like Tuff Green (pictured above at the Mitchell Hotel). A restaurant and club like Tony's Inn could hold community meetings like the Dairy Council's Press Luncheon on June 17, 1955, pictured below. The meeting was in observance of nationwide dairy month. The members of the press were served a meal featuring dairy products. (Both, Memphis Brooks Museum of Art.)

This Hooks Brothers photograph displays the birth of the *Tri-State Defender* on November 3, 1951. The newspaper was founded by journalist and editor Lewis Swingler. Swingler had also edited the *Memphis World* beginning in 1931. Swingler was editor in chief until 1955. During the 1950s, he pushed the paper to cover more civil rights and political topics. This photograph helped to publicize the preview edition of the paper. The front page showcased pictures of Swingler and storylines outlining his direction for the *Tri-State Defender*. The paper was founded as an affiliate of the *Chicago Defender*, a national black newspaper with a long history of promoting civil rights. Swingler intended the Memphis version to follow its lead. He, therefore, widely addressed growing local political activity across the tri-state area, linking these movements to civil rights issues on the national stage. (Department of Art.)

Eight

PRIDE OF PLACE
NEIGHBORHOODS, COMMUNITIES,
AND SOCIAL LIFE

Memphis has always been a city of neighborhood pride. Walker Avenue in south Memphis was home to a residential community that included important social, religious, and educational institutions. Among these were Lemoyne College, Mason Temple, St. Augustine Catholic Church and School, Metropolitan Baptist Church, Second Congregational Church, Lemoyne Gardens, Lelia Walker Club House, and the Four Way Grill. Lemoyne, as it so aptly described itself, was a "Beacon of Hope" for black high school students with aspirations for college. Lemoyne graduated scores of the city's African American leaders during the postwar years. Lemoyne instilled in its students the spirit and practice of social service. The school appointed its first African American president, Hollis Price, in 1943. The freshman class of 1941 did not know that they would endure the hardships of a nation at war, with many of the young men having to interrupt their college years to serve their country, but most pictured here completed their studies and graduated as the proud class of 1945. (Private collection.)

President Hollis Price guided Lemoyne through rapid change and growth during the 1950s. Bruce Hall was built in 1954 at a cost of $375,000. Designed by George Aswumb and Sons, it included an auditorium-gymnasium with seating for 1,600, three basketball courts, a 25-by-75-foot swimming pool, a band room, a drama workshop, a health service center, five classrooms, a kitchen, and a laundry. (Mississippi Valley Collection.)

Bruce Hall was large enough for concerts, dramas, lectures, and basketball. Given the slow pace of integration, it not only became the cultural center of the Walker community, but was also one of the first sites where interracial programs were held. During the 1950s, Lemoyne hosted Leontyne Price, international scholars, Haitian dancers, and Israeli pianists. Before Bruce Hall, most cultural events took place in black churches. (Mississippi Valley Collection.)

Lemoyne influenced the cultural life of the community through outreach programs of groups like the Lemoyne Dance Club, the Lemoyne Choir, and the Lemoyne Drama Group. In 1937, the college was one of only three black colleges to open an art center under the WPA Federal Art Project. Classes were taught in the fine arts and graphic design, and exhibits were shown at the Lemoyne College Federal Art Gallery. The first director of the center was trained muralist Vertis Hayes. Hayes set up the department of art at Lemoyne in 1947. He lived in the community at 964 Florida Street, where he started a small art school. He also started an art program for veterans at the VA hospital. A large mural he painted on the life of George Washington Carver still hangs in the social science building at Jackson State University in Jackson, Mississippi. Reginald Morris taught at Lemoyne during the 1950s. He studied mural painting in Mexico. Morris murals are at Mason Temple and Second Congregational Church on Walker Avenue. The latter artwork features a stunning non-white Jesus. (Above, Mississippi Valley Collection; below, private collection.)

Lemoyne Gardens, the housing project across the street from the college, was also an integral part of the Walker Avenue community. Lemoyne has always been an active part of the surrounding community and at the forefront of service projects. Before construction began on Lemoyne Gardens in 1940, students at the college were asked to carry out tenant surveys and collect data from potential residents. Their findings influenced the selection of the first 580 tenants who moved into the homes. The construction of public housing was problematic since white city leaders often pushed projects over the concerns of black residents whose middle-class homes were destroyed in the process. In the beginning, however, they were intended as a stopgap measure, not a destination. Families lived in public housing with values and aspirations. There were active community leaders, neighborhood associations, and newsletters organized by residents in public housing. Today the housing project no longer exists, replaced by mixed development housing, all part of the extensive renovation of the Walker Avenue neighborhood as home to the legacy of Stax Records. As always, Lemoyne College anchors the revived neighborhood, and the area is now referred to as Soulsville. (Both, Memphis Room.)

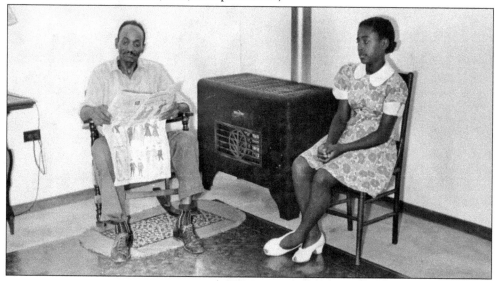

Black middle-class women took on leadership and collaborative roles to sponsor cultural activities. Lelia Walker, pictured at right with her husband, Dr. J. Walker, purchased a residence near Walker Avenue and Mississippi Boulevard for $16,500, donating it to the City Federation of Colored Women's Clubs as a meeting place. Lelia was one of the charter members of Mississippi Boulevard Christian Church. Florence McCleave (below) moved to Memphis after marrying Dr. Benjamin McCleave in 1930. Trained in Rome and France, she was the first African American to perform the title role of Aida in 1927 in Italy. McCleave's most successful pupil was Vera Little, who studied at the Paris Conservatory and had a career with the West Berlin Opera House during the 1960s. Madame McCleave, as black Memphians addressed her, brought concert artists Marian Anderson and Roland Hayes to Memphis. (Both, Memphis Room.)

A variety of sororities and fraternities, art and literary clubs, civic groups, social clubs, and professional organizations sponsored cultural activities. The Alpha Kappa Alpha (AKA) sorority staged eight plays from 1947 to 1957, such as *Life with Father*, *The Barretts of Wimpole Street*, and *The Trial of Mary Durgan* in 1953. The last was put on in Ellis Auditorium, which was integrated in 1949. The play, a courtroom drama about a woman on trial for murdering her lover, was written by Bayard Veiller and was performed on Broadway in 1927. The plays were directed by Ann Reba Twigg and used well-known members of the community. Club activities were well documented in local black newspapers. The scene from the play and the picture of AKA members posing for a shot in the lobby appeared in the *Memphis World* in February 1953. (Both, Memphis Brooks Museum of Art.)

The Sequin Bridge Club, pictured above at its April in Gay Paris formal in 1953 at the Hippodrome, put forth every effort to organize a beautiful affair with a French theme. The Zeta Phi Betas presented *Carmen Jones* at the Ellis Auditorium in May 1953 (below). Black women viewed such cultural expression as a way to uplift black women and challenge negative stereotypes. In their beautiful dresses, high-heeled shoes, tasteful jewelry, and well-coiffed hair, they presented images of African American women that were smart, sexy, strong, and self-respecting. (Both, Memphis Brooks Museum of Art.)

Black women also joined service-oriented organizations like the La Ritas social club and JUGS (Just Us Girls). Members were not wealthy but were part of the new rising black middle class determined to grasp post–World War II opportunities. Black parents encouraged daughters to pursue college degrees to support themselves instead of working in white people's homes or in the service industry. Many were graduates of Lemoyne and were teachers, one of the most respected groups of professionals in the black community. They enjoyed socializing, but club activities were often directed toward the community, particularly children. Lovelle Fouse Jenkins is pictured above (center) as one of the original members of the La Ritas social club and below at Capleville School, one of her first teaching positions in the county. She graduated from Lemoyne with a degree in library science in 1945 and established the library at Ford Road School. (Both, private collection.)

Fashion shows were a popular way for black women to raise funds, collaborate with other organizations to support a diversity of community issues, address the needs of girls and young adults, and encourage cultural activities. This 1959 fashion show, entitled Coiffure, took place at the Hippodrome, which was also used as a skating rink. The large area was decorated with drawings of young fashionable women and elegant street scenes, and was enhanced with jazz music. The contestants were teenagers who were judged on their style of dress and deportment. Each accessorized her gowns with purses, gloves, stockings, and high heels. The hair was carefully done, but make-up appears to have been minimal and tasteful. In 1959, an effort was made for this to be an integrated event, with nine black judges, all female, and two white judges, one male and one female. (Both, Mississippi Valley Collection.)

Wedding portraits were extremely popular with African American women. The Hooks Brothers were called to make everybody's wedding pictures. By the 1940s, the photography studio was run by the sons of Robert and Henry. Cousins Charles and Henry Hooks continued their fathers' tradition of exceptional studio work. They took every social type of photograph imaginable in the African American community. Their technical skill is extremely high, and their work is always focused, compositions are well worked out, and every element is well lighted. Wedding photographs developed into an interesting category where the Hooks Brothers might take formal pictures at the church, create a number of informal scenes leading up to the wedding, and then also take images of the wedding party with friends and family at home. The Wallace-Dancy wedding portrait is featured on the cover (see page 2 for the entire shot). (Both, Mississippi Valley Collection.)

These wedding pictures are of the 1953 Groves-Hayes wedding. Helen Hayes was the granddaughter of Thomas Hayes of Hayes and Sons Funeral Home, the longest-surviving African American business in Memphis. Her father, Thomas Hayes, owned the Birmingham Black Barons. He traded Willie Mays to the New York Giants. Pictures were taken before the wedding, as well as formal shots of the ceremony, wedding party, and family. An unusual addition was a shot of the couple getting into their car, possibly leaving for their honeymoon. (Both, Mississippi Valley Collection.)

An important event of cultural and economic significance during the late 1940s was the construction of a Mason Temple. Work started in 1940 and was completed in 1945 at a cost of $275,679. The building served as the world headquarters of the Church of God in Christ. The temple was 135 feet wide and 200 feet long. (Memphis Room.)

Mason Temple consisted of 24 offices, a pool for baptizing, a nursery, a post office, a barbershop, a beauty shop, dormitory buildings, a cafeteria, and an auditorium. The auditorium was the site of Dr. Martin Luther King Jr.'s "I Have Been to the Mountaintop" speech on April 3, 1968. (Memphis Room.)

Elsie Mason was born in Memphis and was raised in the Church of God in Christ. She worked at the COGIC Saints Industrial and Literary School in Lexington, Mississippi. Elsie also taught school in New York and Memphis. She carried out important fieldwork in Haiti, where she founded the Charles Harrison Mason School. Her faithful devotion to the church included editing the newspaper *Whole Truth* and serving as executive secretary for the COGIC Missions Department. The Hooks Brothers produced this serene and lovely image of Elsie (at right). They also took the group portrait below in 1955 that includes Elsie standing between Bishop Mason and James Patterson. Bishop Mason appointed Patterson bishop and prelate of the Second Ecclesiastical Jurisdiction of Tennessee in 1955. J. O. Patterson was elected first presiding bishop of the Church of God in Christ in 1968. (Right, Pink Palace Museum; below, Mississippi Valley Collection.)

During the 1950s, Hooks Brothers was invited into the Mason home to take pictures. Intimate interior scenes of individual homes were a Hooks Brothers staple. In segregated Memphis, scenes of the homes of black middle-class Memphians were rarely viewed outside of that social context. Mason appears inviting but always the humble man he was known to be. He allowed Hooks Brothers to take pictures of each room in his home, including the bedrooms. (Both, Memphis Room.)

Another important community in south Memphis was founded along Bellevue Boulevard and South Parkway East. Inez Jenkins Glenn was a wife and mother, an active community leader, and an educator in her south Memphis neighborhood. She was born in 1899 in Hernando, Mississippi. She first taught in Mississippi schools after being certified to teach in 1931. She became a teacher like her father, Sam Jenkins. Sam, born into slavery in Mississippi in 1855, taught school in Desoto County. Inez moved to Memphis after her marriage, some time during the 1930s, to 1388 Hemlock Street. Historically, this area has been settled by African Americans since the beginning of the 20th century. (Both, Wilford Glenn Collection.)

Like many rural African Americans migrating to Memphis from the country, Glenn maintained extensive vegetable and flower gardens, and grew turkeys, chickens, grapes for wine, and so forth. She started a flower business that she ran from her home. She sent her son, Wilford Glenn, to a private kindergarten for black children. Rosebud School was located behind Second Congregational Church near Walker and McDowell Streets. Wilford is pictured in the lower right in each photograph. The female principal, teacher, and minister are unidentified. According to oral interviews, Rosebud was a very good school. The building no longer exists, but effective learning was accomplished here. (Both, Wilford Glenn Collection.)

The Glenn family joined Greenwood CME Church when they came to Memphis. It started out as a Bush Arbor Church on the outskirts of the city, first near Ropers Alley, then Greenwood Station. Today this is Lamar Avenue and Bellevue Boulevard. They asked to meet in old Greenwood School, then located near Heistan Place. The early members decided to name the church Greenwood CME in gratitude to the school and the neighborhood. In 1916, members had saved enough to purchase a lot to construct the first church. It was completed in 1920 at 1066 South Bellevue Boulevard. In church records, Inez Glenn is listed as one of the most active members during the late 1920s and 1930s. The church has since moved to its present site at 3311 Kimball Avenue. Greenwood CME Church is one of the largest of its denomination in the region. It hosted the funeral services of author Alex Haley on February 10, 1992. The style of the photograph appears to be that of Hooks Brothers, and it is dated to about 1937. (Wilford Glenn Collection.)

Inez Glenn (pictured above, standing beneath the lightbulb) assumed a leadership role in her community. From the perspective of the black church, community outreach was also considered part of an individual's spiritual service and growth. Glenn worked extensively with the South Side Community Club, which she managed as club president for many years. She invited groups and individuals like the black health care professionals pictured here to teach classes in health and to demonstrate proper care for the sick. For short periods of time, Glenn worked outside of the home when she was employed at Mammoth Life and Accident Insurance Company, a black insurance company located on Beale Street. Glenn's life experience was typical of many mature African American women during the postwar years. They led hardworking, full lives within family, home, friends, church, and community. Glenn is pictured below in the second row, third from the left. (Both, Wilford Glenn Collection.)

Neighborhood schools like Hamilton, Booker T. Washington, and Manassas High Schools were centers of pride that also anchored their communities. Booker T. Washington was led by Blair T. Hunt for 25 years without an assistant principal. Booker T. Washington High School became the first black high school in Memphis in 1926. Hunt was appointed principal in 1932. At the time he assumed leadership, it had an enrollment of 1,600 students. (Mississippi Valley Collection.)

Hunt immediately began to improve the school, adding six new rooms and securing WPA funds to build the city's first athletic field for black students. He also improved physical facilities by adding a field house for athletes and sports equipment. He enlarged the school's shops and the building that served as the instrumental music department. (Memphis Room.)

Hunt diversified the curriculum by increasing the number of electives. He then added guidance counseling services to help students make the best choices about their studies. He continued to improve the school throughout his tenure. The school enrollment grew to about 2,000 students at its height. Hunt maintained discipline and order with an iron hand and succeeded because he loved his students and they knew it. He inherited a handmade brass bell from his predecessor that was his inseparable symbol of authority. The Booker T. Washington motto was "We Lead and Others Follow." These pictures depict students in the library and wood shop class. (Both, Memphis Room.)

There was a diversity of extracurricular activities available. About 70 percent of the student population participated in the activities program. Students took pride in their work on the school paper, the *Washingtonian*, and the school annual, the *Warrior*. There were also essay contests and the "Quiz 'em on the Air" team. The Booker T. Washington Band was the pride and joy of the school. Washington's teaching philosophy emphasized sound values, including cleanliness, honesty, and responsibility. Booker T. Washington's auditorium and cafeteria were often used for community meetings, such as this one (pictured below) in the school cafeteria in 1944. The woman standing to the right is famous gospel composer Lucie B. Campbell, who was a teacher of English and American history at her alma mater for 42 years. (Both, Memphis Room.)

Hamilton High School was the pride of the community it served. By the end of the 1930s, its predecessor, old Greenwood, was overcrowded. It also lacked adequate sanitary facilities, heating, and running water. Rapid population growth south of McLemore Avenue extending to Person Street city limits was the real factor. Since 1922, new subdivisions had developed southward, including Pillow and Bradshaw, West Dixie Heights, Nicholson, and South Dixie Heights. In 1940, the school board purchased 14 acres from a "colored" farmer named Philip Nicholson and planned a new school on Kerr Avenue and Wilson Street. The decision was then made to rename old Greenwood in honor of the respected educator and author Green Polonius Hamilton. As the old school graduated it last eighth-grade class at the Melrose Street location, Hamilton opened in 1941. This school picture dates from 1949. (Memphis Room.)

Completed at a cost of $204,136.44, the new school opened at 1478 Wilson Street with James Buckner as principal. It was made up of grades one through eight. One grade was added each year until it was a four-year high school with the beginning 1945–1946 school year. This meant that students in the south Memphis area would now have their own neighborhood high school. The last class at Greenwood was disappointed they would not have graduation exercises but were reminded that they would forever be recognized as the "firsts." Pictured below are students in a music class in 1943. The teacher is possibly Lucille Rhine. (Both, Memphis Room.)

As the big day approached when the new school would graduate its first senior class, Hamiltonians had an outstanding year. The two-year-old football team won the city's Negro League Football Championship, and the students held their first senior prom. School leaders decided that Hamilton and Manassas would share graduation exercises. The event was to take place at Mason Temple, the crowning glory of the Church of God in Christ, just completed in 1945 with a new auditorium that could seat 9,000 people. The biggest surprise for the students was the guest speaker, the highly esteemed Mary McLeod Bethune, an individual whose picture was posted in every black high school along with Harriet Tubman, Booker T. Washington, Frederick Douglass, and Abraham Lincoln as heroic figures to emulate. On May 23, 1946, Mary McLeod Bethune spoke to 33 graduating seniors. Thirteen of those graduating had attended school together since third grade. Hooks Brothers photographed the event, recording the famous lady's arrival at Union Station and the group of honored black community leaders that welcomed Mary McLeod Bethune to Memphis. (Memphis Room.)

Manassas High School in north Memphis continued to grow under the administration of Ashton B. Hayes (standing to the right of Mary McLeod Bethune). A respected educator and civic leader, Hayes was an excellent role model, helping students to continue with college education or pursue other areas of training. By the 1950s, when the school board required all principals hold a master's degree in education, he graciously moved aside for a younger principal. However, since the experience of educators like Hayes was always in demand, he served as principal of Lester Elementary School before retiring in 1955. (Right, Memphis Room; below, Mississippi Valley Collection.)

Porter Elementary School had an equally proud tradition. When Benjamin Hooks, a future leader of the NAACP, attended in the 1930s, he described it as an excellent school with teachers recruited by principal Lawyer Brown. They sang "Lift Every Voice and Sing" each day, followed by the Lord's Prayer and a Christian hymn. Black history was already part of the curriculum. They also learned invaluable lessons about how to survive in a system where whites controlled the government, economy, and law. By the 1940s and 1950s, Porter was still serving its students and community with the same loyalty. Above, Professor Brown, the faculty, and the entire student body proudly stand in front of their school and neighborhood in 1943. Below is a picture of the eighth-grade class from 1943. (Both, Memphis Room.)

The wider community also supported academic activities. In 1956, Floyd Bass Jr. of LaRose won first place in the 28th annual spelling bee for black children sponsored by the city newspaper, the *Press Scimitar*. Vahness Moore of Hamilton was in second place, and Magnolia McKoy from Shelby County Training School was third. The spelling bee was held at Booker T. Washington High School with a concert by the 50-piece Geeter High School Band, directed by David Newburn and broadcast over WREC radio. The school below is not identified. It may be Cummings Junior High School. The students are stunning in their black and white attire, set off by their neat, proud carriage. (Both, Mississippi Valley Collection.)

Universal Life was one of the best-known success stories of the postwar period. Black capitalist Dr. J. E. Walker founded the insurance company in 1923.Universal Life prospered into a multi-million-dollar enterprise. Universal Life was a household word in the insurance business. In 1947, it became the second African American company in the United States to achieve million-dollar-capital status. (Memphis Room.)

In 1950, success enabled Universal Life to move into a new building designed by African American architects McKissack and McKissack, the first African American architectural firm in Tennessee. The beautiful, Egyptian-inspired building still stands at Linden Avenue and Danny Thomas Boulevard. Every step of the company's success and its major move to its new building was documented by Hooks Brothers photographers. (Memphis Room.)

The interior offices were as beautifully photographed as the exterior. The emphasis was on a modern, clean look that showed the equipment, space, professional atmosphere, and employees off to their best advantage. The auditing department boasted 5,000 square feet of working space. The equipment was the most up-to-date for speed and efficiency. The employees at the home office in Memphis were divided into 17 groups. There were 31 agency offices in the eight states Universal Life served. Most of the office workers were women. (Both, Memphis Room.)

Dr. Walker (pictured above, center) established Tri-State Bank with his son, A. Maceo Walker, in 1946 at 392 Beale Street. This was the same site where Robert Church Sr. founded the first black bank in Memphis, Solvent Savings Bank and Trust, in 1906. Note the advertisement for the black newspaper the *Tri-State Defender*, which relocated its offices to 164 Beale Street. Dr. Walker is pictured standing in front of the site, which is on the National Register of Historic Places. Much of the bank's success was due to the new CPA and army officer Walker hired named Jesse Turner. He was a political activist, and during the civil rights era, the bank was a meeting place for local leaders. Bank officials often kept the vaults open late into the night to provide protestors with bail money. Today Tri-State Bank, with five branches, is one of the largest black-owned businesses in Tennessee. (Above, Department of Art; below, Memphis Room.)

Dr. Walker's influence extended to philanthropy and community service. In 1952, Walker was honored for his work to improve housing conditions for black Memphians. The ceremony celebrated the ground-breaking for the Walker Homes subdivision. Walker's motivation was that building a black subdivision for 1,500 black families was a much better financial and social investment in the community and the city than another housing project. Dr. Walker is seated to the right, looking out over the crowd of almost 6,000 in attendance. Walker Homes is located in southwest Memphis. It was a major community project that deserved recognition, but it also reflected the strength of an entrenched segregationist environment where whites avidly protested the efforts of blacks to move into available housing in white neighborhoods. (Memphis Brooks Museum of Art.)

Toward the end of the 1950s, the tradition of black and white collaboration on a number of community projects continued, but younger African Americans were becoming less tolerant of segregated facilities and public spaces. An example is the first institution in Tennessee dedicated to the care of neglected and dependent African American children. The agency was the vision of community members John A. Parsons, Russell Doss, Rev. Samuel A. Owen, Rev. J. A. McDaniel, and Dr. Hollis Price. From the beginning, it attracted the interest of WDIA, known as the "Goodwill Station" because of its widespread service to the black community. The white owner of the station, Bert Ferguson, as well as the entire staff, supported the project with a pledge of $40,000. As a result, the facility was named Goodwill Homes for Children, Inc. African American contractor Edgar H. Davis won the bid to build the homes and entered a $1,000 donation of his own. Goodwill Homes was well constructed out of concrete and brick, incorporating space for 22 children. (Mississippi Valley Collection.)

Mildred T. Heard was selected as the first executive director of the Goodwill Homes for Children. A graduate of Lemoyne College, she earned a Master of Arts degree in sociology from Atlanta University. Heard help set up the Child Welfare Division at the Tennessee Department of Public Welfare. She was married to J. Heard, a professional baseball player with the Baltimore Orioles in the Pacific Coast League. She is pictured below with the first 11 children to live at Goodwill Homes on their way to Geeter School. In the background is Audrey M. Williams, the supervising housemother. (Both, Mississippi Valley Collection.)

Goodwill Homes was a one-level structure with space for 22 children. One of the buildings was for boys and the other for girls. Every attempt was made to make the space feel like a home rather than an institution. Children were allowed to have pets, as shown in this 1965 photograph. In the same year, the home was raising funds to add 16 more spaces. Judge Kenneth Turner of Juvenile Court was chairman of the drive to raise $100,000 to enable the home to care for 38 children. He is shown below with Jaqueline Hilliard (left) and Annie Ruth Dockery. Today the program is known as Goodwill Homes Community Services, Inc. Having enlarged its mission to address issues of poverty by empowering others to become self-sufficient, it provides extensive social services in southwest Memphis. (Both, Mississippi Valley Collection.)

During the 1950s, T. O. Fuller Park operated as a segregated recreational space for African Americans. Fuller Park was the first state park for African Americans established east of the Mississippi River. It was founded in 1933 and was named after Rev. T. O. Fuller. It is located in southwest Memphis on Mitchell Avenue and encompasses about 1,500 acres. The new park was originally called Shelby City Negro State Park. It was allegedly the site where Hernando de Soto first saw the Mississippi River. However, the land was never particularly valued for its scenic appeal, which may have factored into its selection as recreational space suitable for African Americans. A Native American village and burial mounds were unearthed in 1939 during the initial park development. Construction was interrupted while University of Tennessee archaeologists investigated the site. The excavation, referred to as the Fuller Mounds Project, continued until the start of World War II. When excavations resumed in 1952, the mounds were reclassified as nonsegregated and renamed Chucalissa Archaeological State Park, a nonsegregated "Indian" space within a segregated park built for "Negroes." (Mississippi Valley Collection.)

After World War II, African Americans began to complain about the lack of facilities at the park. After the discovery of Native American mounds, little had been constructed on the site. The acidity of the water eroded pipes. Thousands of people would come out to the park, and there would be no running water. Memphis Light, Gas, and Water never wired the camp for electrical power because papers had not been signed in Nashville. In addition, the dining hall had small windows and lacked ventilation, making the building very hot. Although many groups had used the park, African Americans were looking for other facilities. As a result, about 20 new buildings were constructed as part of a new camp, as well as bleachers, shelters, boat docks, and a new dining hall large enough to accommodate about 140 people. Pictured here is the new dining hall area. (Mississippi Valley Collection.)

In 1955, pool construction finally began at T. O. Fuller State Park. It also acquired a bathhouse, a lodge, athletic fields, hiking trails, a concession building, and picnic areas. In 1956, the city built a segregated golf course on the site. Over time, T. O. Fuller State Park has become a recreation site for all. It is well maintained and attracts visitors to the Chucalissa Museum with its exhibits and sites interpreted by local Native Americans. As a state park, it offers a unique interpretation of Native American and African American history and culture. (Mississippi Valley Collection.)

As Memphis inched toward integration of its public facilities, problems surfaced concerning the city's long struggle to provide health care for its black citizens. John Gaston Hospital, the public hospital that served a majority of black patients, treated them in a separate ward with separate staff. The NAACP took a hard-line position against the construction of a new segregated hospital, which they saw as reinforcing the status quo. Local leaders believed that the need for a modern health facility for blacks was critical, integrated or not. Memphis leaders and the NAACP held a meeting concerning integration at Metropolitan Baptist Church. Hooks Brothers photographed (from left to right) Dr. Hollis Price, president of Lemoyne College; Walter White, executive secretary of the NAACP in New York; and Utillus Phillips, president of the local branch of the NAACP, standing in front of the church on Walker Avenue. Attorney Harold Flowers of Pine Bluff, Arkansas, was the guest speaker. He discussed the struggle to integrate schools in Arkansas. The photograph appeared in the *Memphis World* on June 24, 1952. (Memphis Brooks Museum of Art.)

At old John Gaston Hospital, more than 6,000 babies a year, mostly African American, were born absent of a nursing viewing area or father's waiting room. There were not even chairs to sit in. Most people had to bring expectant mothers to the hospital and leave. When fathers and family wanted to see the newborns, they had to wait outside the nursery until they caught the attention of a nurse. She would bring the baby to the door, where one had to look through glass and metal mesh. These are pictures of John Gaston and the small maternity ward annex built in 1937. (Both, Memphis Room.)

In 1953, work started on the E. H. Crump Memorial Hospital for Negroes. A joint project of city and county governments, it was completed in March 1956. City leaders had struggled for the past 17 years to construct a teaching hospital for black physicians and nurses. It was built at a cost of $2 million and contained 128 beds. The building's seven stories towered above Jefferson Avenue and Dunlap Street. A nurses' home was attached to the rear with space for 66 students, as well as space for 10 resident interns to live. Architects Eason, Anthony, McKinnie, and Cox designed the building. Bass, O'Brien, and Padgett were the general contractors. The photograph below depicts Mayor Edmund Orgill speaking at the dedication ceremonies on March 19, 1956. (Both, Mississippi Valley Collection.)

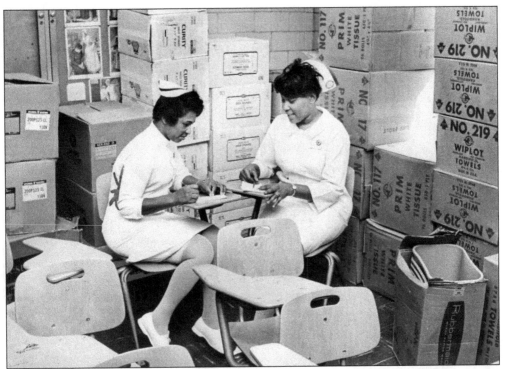

In 1968, renovations began to turn Crump into a women's hospital. During the renovations, the old private hospital for blacks was used as a teaching unit for the University of Tennessee Center for the Health Sciences (UTCHS) and also served as a general hospital. These images show the cramped quarters nurses had to maneuver in while all the changes were taking place. (Both, Mississippi Valley Collection.)

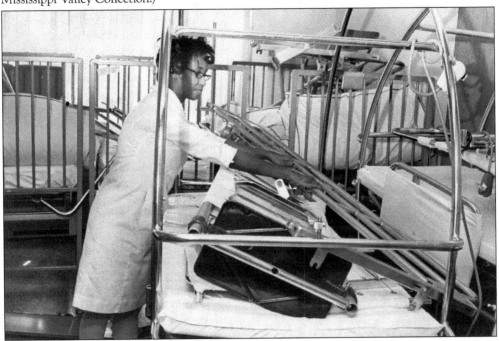

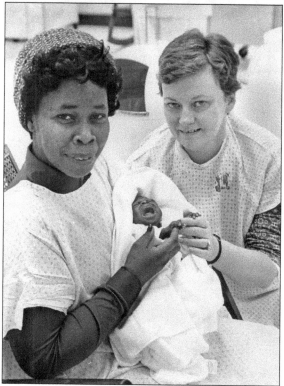

E. Crump Women's Hospital and Perinatal Facility opened in 1977, including a newborn center specializing in the care of premature and severely ill babies. The hospital, once restricted to serving only blacks, is now dedicated to serving women. Above is a picture of Dr. Wheeler Lipes (left) and Dr. Preston Dilts outside the new nursery. They noted that the new hospital has been designed with the entire family in mind, with a large nursery with a skylight and a waiting room for fathers and one for family as well. (Mississippi Valley Collection.)

Mrs. Willie B. Burt is pictured with social worker Lynn Jackson and her newborn son, Lamrio Burt. He weighed 2 pounds, 14 ounces at birth in February 1978 and spent the first few months of his life in the Newborn Center at E. Crump Women's Hospital. (Mississippi Valley Collection.)

BIBLIOGRAPHY

Bond, Beverly G. and Janann Sherman. *Memphis in Black and White*. Charleston, SC: Arcadia
    Publishing, 2003.
Church, Roberta and Ronald Walter. Charles Crawford, ed. *Nineteenth Century Memphis Families
    of Color: 1850–1900*. Memphis, TN: Murdock Printing Company, 1987.
DeCosta-Willis, Miriam. *Notable Black Memphians*. Amherst, NY: Cambria Press, 2008.
Hamilton, G. P. *The Bright Side of Memphis*. Memphis, TN: G. P. Hamilton, 1908.
Green, Laurie B. *Battling the Plantation Mentality: Memphis and the Black Freedom Struggle*. Chapel
    Hill, NC: University of North Carolina Press, 2007.
Hooks, Benjamin L., with Jerry Guess. *The March for Civil Rights: The Benjamin Hooks Story*.
    Chicago: ABA Publishing, 2004.
Lamon, Lester C. *Blacks in Tennessee 1791–1970*. Knoxville, TN: University of Tennessee Press,
    1981.
Lee, George W. *Beale Street: Where the Blues Began*. New York: Robert O. Ballou, 1934.
Pacini, Marina and David McCarthy, eds. *Photographs from the Memphis World 1949–1964*.
    Memphis, TN: Memphis Brooks Museum of Art, 2008.
Tucker, David M. *Black Pastors and Leaders: Memphis, 1819–1972*. Memphis, TN: Memphis State
    University Press, 1975.
———. *Lieutenant Lee of Beale Street*. Nashville, TN: Vanderbilt University Press, 1971.

Visit us at
arcadiapublishing.com

Printed in the USA
CPSIA information can be obtained
at www.ICGtesting.com
LVHW081745200923
758542LV00024B/50

9 781531 644376